# God I need to talk to You about Dishonesty

Michael Newman

CONCORDIA PUBLISHING HOUSE · SAINT LOUIS

3558 S. Jefferson Avenue, St. Louis, MO 63118-3968
1-800-325-3040 · www.cph.org



Written by Michael Newman



Manufactured in the United States of America

1 2 3 4 5 6 7 8 9 10 22 21 20 19 18 17 16 15 14 13

# Table of CONTENTS

A note to the reader: Some of the details in these prayers may not reflect your unique situation. Therefore, we encourage you to adapt them where appropriate to fit your circumstances and spiritual needs.

# Introduction

A little white lie. A fib. Bending the truth. Embellishing. There are many ways to describe what we do that take the sting out of the sin of lying. But we know that a lie is a lie, regardless of its size or the label we attach to it.

The first lie was told in the Garden of Eden when the serpent twisted the truth of God's words. People have been lying ever since. It's easy. It's safe. Well, at least it feels that way when we aren't willing to tell the truth, when we're embarrassed or uncomfortable with total honesty, when a little white lie seems like the best way to handle something that makes us feel awkward.

So, what if we were to examine our motivation for lying and whether that motivation is better than simple honesty? Does it really help our friend when we say that her new hair color is flattering? Does covering up illegal or immoral behavior ever, ever pay?

The news is full of stories of celebrities who have lived lies and then been caught in their deceit. While the secular world has become increasingly accepting of ungodly behavior, it still abhors a liar. But big lies, like drug use or extramarital affairs, and little lies, like what time you got back from lunch or whether a friend's new poem is good, all fall into the same category of sin. A lie is a lie. And God abhors sin.

The beautiful truth in our dishonest world is that Jesus is the way, the truth, and the life. Jesus offers forgiveness and mercy to every liar, even to us, even to the famous people, regardless of motivation, because Jesus took all sin with Him to the cross. When we recognize our dishonesty and repent of it, Jesus is there with His arms outstretched to receive us.

And that's the truth.

# Accidental Dishonesty

Dear God,

I don't get up in the morning intending to lie. I just don't like to reveal too much about myself. I do not like to be vulnerable. I like my privacy. Today my friend told me that I hurt her feelings because I didn't tell the truth about where I was last night. Honestly, I didn't want to tell her. What was I supposed to do? I thought her feelings might be hurt if she knew what I was doing. I also thought she might disapprove of whom I was with.

Now I'm in trouble. My friend is angry with me. This is all very confusing. If I tell the truth, I'm in trouble. And if I don't tell the truth, I'm in trouble.

I need help to sort this out. What should I do, God? I know that being dishonest is wrong, but sometimes I have to lie—at least I feel like I have to lie.

Dear God, Your Son said that He is the way and the truth and the life. I need Him to show me the way so I can live in the truth. I need His help. I know You sent Jesus to save me. Please help me through this complicated mess.

## Something to think about

Make me to know Your ways, O Lord; teach me Your paths. Lead me in Your truth and teach me, for You are the God of my salvation; for You I wait all the day long.

Psalm 25:4–5

# Trying to Look Better

Dear God,

I did it again. I didn't want to be embarrassed at work, so I exaggerated when I told someone about some of my job experience. I also criticized another co-worker so I would look better. The criticism wasn't the whole truth.

All I wanted was a chance at a better opportunity. It seems like I'm always being left out and never get a break. I want my boss to know that I have talent. I know I can do a good job.

But I hope this doesn't hurt my chances. I don't think anyone will find out, but I feel guilty about what I did. I seem to be caught in a pattern of dishonesty. Before I can stop it, a lie comes out of my mouth. I know my co-worker isn't all that great. Some of what I said was true. It isn't fair that she gets away with everything but still gets so many new opportunities. I can't stand back and do nothing, can I?

Maybe that's what I need to do. I remember being taught that I need to trust You, God. Please help me do that. I know You love me. I know I'm Your child. Help me to be silent and to trust that You will take care of me.

## Something to think about

Trust in the LORD with all your heart, and do not lean on your own understanding. In all your ways acknowledge Him, and He will make straight your paths.

Proverbs 3:5–6

# The Truth

Dear God,

My mother sat me down today and told me I have a problem with being truthful. It was after she found out that I lied about going to a party last night. She told me that I'm not even aware of when I am being dishonest, that I say untruthful things before I realize I'm lying. She told me that this habit has to stop because it is hurting others and it's hurting me. She told me that she doesn't trust me very much anymore.

I'm angry about this, God. Everything I say isn't a lie. I've done plenty of things to prove that I'm trustworthy. This really hurts.

But I think my mom is right. I hate to admit it, but my lying has caused a lot of trouble lately. I know I have to stop. When my mom talked to me, she gave me a piece of paper with a Bible verse from the Psalms written on it: "Send out Your light and Your truth; let them lead me" (Psalm 43:3).

I need You to lead me to be more truthful.

I need You to shed some light on this struggle, God. It used to be hard for me to cross the line of dishonesty, but I've told so many lies that now the line seems to be gone. Sometimes I even believe what isn't true. Please help me. I know You want me to be honest. Please teach me.

### Something to think about

Behold, You delight in truth in the inward being, and You teach me wisdom in the secret heart.

Psalm 51:6

# Fatigue

Dear God,

Living in lies is exhausting. At work I have to be careful about what I say to whom. At home I have to keep track of the cover stories I use. At church I have to remember whom I was talking to about whom. I can't even remember all the reasons I give for ignoring certain people's phone calls and e-mails.

This has to stop. I'm done living in constant deception. I'm going to ask for help. Someone at church who has been like a grandparent to me has offered to take me out to lunch. I'm going to see if this person may be my source of help and accountability. A little wisdom and encouragement would help too.

Thank You for showing me that I'm not in this alone, God. Thank You for providing an open door for some help and guidance. I need a new beginning. I realize that my dishonesty is rooted in some of my own destructive behaviors. Sometimes I want to avoid conflict.

Sometimes I am trying to cover up what I know is wrong. Sometimes I'm just afraid of hurting someone's feelings or of someone knowing that I don't measure up.

Please rescue me from this draining and wearying pattern of lies. I'm ready to change.

## Something to think about

The Lord is near to all who call on Him, to all who call on Him in truth.

Psalm 145:18

# A New Day

## Dear God,

You bring the gift of truth to my life. You did that by sending Your Son, Jesus. Thank You for blessing me with such a reliable source of truth. Thank You for clearing up my confused judgment by giving me a Savior who reveals truth to me. I need Him. I need His gracious guidance.

Today I will listen to Him before I speak. My new mentor gave me this verse from the Book of Proverbs: "What a person desires is unfailing love; better to be poor than a liar" (Proverbs 19:22 NIV).

The verse is so true! Some of my dishonesty happens because I don't want someone to be mad at me or I want someone to like me more. I'm looking for unfailing love. I realize now that I don't have to lie or tell half-truths in order to get people to love me. My true value is in Jesus Christ. Your love is what I need. And Your love is what I have.

I also realize that I'm dishonest because I'm doing the wrong things—things that make me feel guilty. I need Your help to live in obedience to You—not because I'm afraid, but because I'm grateful. You keep loving me and caring for me even when I fail. Thank You. Thank You for never letting me go.

### Something to think about

And the Word became flesh and dwelt among us, and we have seen His glory, glory as of the only Son from the Father, full of grace and truth. . . . For the law was given through Moses; grace and truth came through Jesus Christ.

John 1:14, 17

# Serving Others

Dear God,

Over the past few days, I've realized that my lack of truth-telling has hurt people in my life. The untrue things I've said about others have wounded them. Hiding what I'm doing pushes people away from me and makes them feel unwanted and uncared for.

I think I've been so busy protecting myself that I haven't noticed the hurt I've caused in others. But I see now that the hurt is deep. I know I can't undo everything I've done, but I know You can create a new heart in me. I know You can give me a new beginning. I know You can work forgiveness—in me and in others. Today, I ask You to fill me with peace and strength: peace to be silent when I am tempted to speak falsely and strength to prevail when the temptation to do wrong tries to overwhelm me.

I know that my honesty will grow as I listen to You, follow You, serve You, and serve others.

You are my Savior, Lord. You make me a new creation through Jesus' work for me.

## Something to think about

The Lord is merciful and gracious, slow to anger and abounding in steadfast love. . . . As far as the east is from the west, so far does He remove our transgressions from us. As a father shows compassion to his children, so the Lord shows compassion to those who fear Him.

Psalm 103:8, 12–13

# Secrets

Dear God,

What do I do with my secrets? I've hidden a lot from everyone in my life. My struggle is that I can't hide them from myself. My mentor told me that some of my secrets need to be told, but I can wait to tell them at the right time. There's no need to rush.

That's a relief. I don't want to hurt anyone else right now.

But I know I can never reveal some of the secrets that bother me and make me guilty. I never want anyone to know. It wouldn't do anyone any good. My mentor told me that I can confess these secrets to You. She said that You will hear me and forgive me. She told me that Jesus died for these secrets a long time ago, so they're no surprise to Him. She said that You will carry these burdens for me.

That is a big relief. I can't keep thinking about all the things I've done and all the lies I've spoken to cover up the truth. Maybe one day I'll confess these to my pastor, too. My mentor said I can do that. She told me that he would keep them in confidence and speak God's words of forgiveness to me. I may do that one day. But, for now, I'll speak them to You and ask You to carry them for me so I can be free to start a new and honest life.

Thank You for loving me so much that You listen to me and forgive me.

## Something to think about

If we say we have no sin, we deceive ourselves, and the truth is not in us. If we confess our sins, He is faithful and just to forgive us our sins and to cleanse us from all unrighteousness.

1 John 1:8–9

# A Challenging Journey

Dear God,

This is really difficult. Living honestly takes a remarkable amount of energy and self-control—at least it seems that way right now. I know I'm just beginning this journey, but I'm finding that I need to live differently. On one hand, I need to be very deliberate and take my time when I speak. My reflex is to cover up the truth, so I need to think about how to speak honestly. On the other hand, I need to trust people to be compassionate when I do speak. If I admit a mistake or a wrong, I have to believe that people will be forgiving. Even if they're not, I have to trust that saying "I'm sorry" is better than speaking a lie.

Honesty is a challenging journey. But I know it is not too difficult for You, dear Savior. I do not take this journey depending on my strength, but on Yours. I will not be afraid of what may result from my honesty. I will trust in You. You save me from dishonesty. You restore my soul and walk with me in every moment.

I will move forward one step at a time in Your care. I will come to You in prayer as I consider every decision and every thought. I know You hear my prayers and will lead me faithfully.

### Something to think about

Behold, God is my salvation; I will trust, and will not be afraid; for the Lord God is my strength and my song, and He has become my salvation.

Isaiah 12:2

# The Little Things

Dear God,

Thank You for Your strength and guidance. Thank You for giving me a new beginning and filling me with Your strength to live in the truth. Thank You for Your kindness and forgiveness. I know I don't deserve it. I am awed by Your love and restoration.

I've seen You at work in my life as I confront my dishonesty. You have been showing me that I can live in the truth and speak the truth. But I still need Your help. It's easy to brush aside the little things. It is easy to be dishonest about whether someone's new hairstyle or outfit is flattering. Bringing office supplies home from work for my personal use is a small act that is easy to let slide.

Help me with these little things. I know I can't be perfect, but I don't want to slip into dishonesty. I don't want to live a life that is filled with hidden shame. I know You take care of the big things. Please extend Your grace into every corner of my life so I can give You glory in all I do—even in the little things.

### Something to think about

And God is able to make all grace abound to you, so that having all sufficiency in all things at all times, you may abound in every good work.

2 Corinthians 9:8

# Hypocrisy

Dear God,

I feel like a hypocrite! I'm trying to be "good." I'm trying to be "nice." I feel like I'm not being myself! It gets so discouraging when every fiber of my being seems to pull me back to acting like the old me.

I visited with my mentor today. She is so wise. She told me that a hypocrite pretends to do what she doesn't want to do. I'm not doing that, she said. I'm growing into the person Jesus calls me to be. By God's grace, I'm trying to adopt a new pattern in life. Even if it means going through the motions, I'm practicing doing what is right. The Holy Spirit is shaping me as a follower of Jesus.

Thank You for her words. I know it will take a while before being honest feels "normal." Please hold on to me as I adjust. Help me to believe that my family and friends are supporting me every step of the way. You have surrounded me with people who show Your love. I know there are people who may never trust me again, but lead me to be encouraged by the people who are giving me another chance. Provide Your sustaining help through those who offer me Your unconditional love.

### Something to think about

I have been crucified with Christ. It is no longer I who live, but Christ who lives in me. And the life I now live in the flesh I live by faith in the Son of God, who loved me and gave Himself for me.

Galatians 2:20

# The Way

## Dear God,

In Jesus, You are the way and the truth and the life. You have saved me and forgiven me. Because of Your work through the beautiful cross of Jesus and His resurrection, I am a new creation. I am in awe at Your unconditional love for me. I am truly blessed by Your care in my life.

My dishonesty has been wrong and shameful. My lies have made a mess of my life and have disappointed You and others. I am so sorry for my poor choices. I am deeply sorry for the way I've chosen to cover up my wrongdoing.

Thank You for giving me another chance. Thank You for being the way, the truth, and the life in my journey. I wouldn't know what to do or how to live unless You showed me my new path and gave me Your Spirit to move along it.

Please fill each moment of my life with

Your strength and direction. Please make Your thoughts my thoughts and Your words my words. In every small conversation and action, help me live in truth and speak the truth. Form me into a kind and honest person, dear Savior.

## Something to think about

For to this you have been called, because Christ also suffered for you, leaving you an example, so that you might follow in His steps. . . . He Himself bore our sins in His body on the tree, that we might die to sin and live to righteousness. By His wounds you have been healed. For you were straying like sheep, but have now returned to the Shepherd and Overseer of your souls.

1 Peter 2:21, 24–25

# A Test

Dear God,

Today I was asked to go to a party with some people from work. I knew it would not be the best place to go, so, instead of being pressured to say yes, or making up an excuse—a lie—about why I couldn't hang out, I told the truth. In a gentle way, I simply said that it wouldn't be the best thing for me to do right now.

An amazing thing happened: my co-worker simply answered, "Okay." She wasn't mad. She wasn't insulted. She even smiled and said, "Maybe next time."

I felt so free after this surprising conversation. I knew I wasn't going to do something I would regret and feel the need to cover up. I also knew that I wouldn't have to remember the fake story I told my co-worker. Most of all, I realized that I can be honest. I can actually live a life that helps me be a person of truth.

Clearly, this was an answer to prayer, God. Thank You for coming through with the words

I needed to speak and the strength I needed to stay on Your course. This victory gives me hope. I believe I can be truthful. I am eager to pursue this new path. It's all because of You and Your grace in my life. Thank You!

## Something to think about

No temptation has overtaken you that is not common to man. God is faithful, and He will not let you be tempted beyond your ability, but with the temptation He will also provide the way of escape, that you may be able to endure it.

1 Corinthians 10:13

# A Victory

Dear God,

I want to thank You for another victory today!

My boss asked me if I felt I was qualified to tackle a project at work. He mentioned that if there was someone who I believed could help me out, I could let him know and he would form a team to get the work done. In the past, I would have exaggerated my qualifications in order to try to impress him and outdo my co-workers. Not today. Today I let him know honestly what I understood and was able to do. I also recommended a co-worker who has some key skills I don't have.

I think my boss was impressed. He seemed very pleased that I was honest about my own capabilities and that I recognized the talents of someone else. I got the feeling that he respected me as a professional and that he believed I was genuinely interested in the success of the company.

What an amazing sensation it was to feel respected by him! He smiled and went along with my recommendation. Honesty about my weaknesses actually seemed to take me farther ahead than dishonesty about my talents and qualifications.

This is a good path, dear Savior. Thank You for giving me positive reinforcement for my new life of honesty. Even when I'm afraid to live in a new way, You give me courage and new reasons to keep walking with You.

## Something to think about

Humble yourselves, therefore, under the mighty hand of God so that at the proper time He may exalt you, casting all your anxieties on Him, because He cares for you.

1 Peter 5:6–7

# A Close Call

## Dear God,

I experienced a close call today. There is a person at church who really gets on my nerves. We've never seen eye to eye, and she has not been particularly kind to me. To be completely honest, I haven't been very kind to her either.

A friend sent me a text about this person today. It was the latest update on some of her annoying behavior. I almost sent a text back with a juicy piece of gossip, but I didn't do it. I didn't want to step back into a dark and dishonest life in the shadows. The prospect of sending an ugly text back struck me as repulsive and unappealing. I know I felt this way because You are changing my heart. Thank You for rescuing me.

In the past, I would have sent a text back right away. I would have added embellished rumors to the conversation. I would have had to hide behind fake talk at church when I saw her, or I would have had to avoid her. But I'm free of that today, thanks to You.

I like this life much better than my old life. O Savior, please continue to give me a new heart. Please lead me to love doing the right thing.

### Something to think about

Create in me a clean heart, O God, and renew a right spirit within me. Cast me not away from Your presence, and take not Your Holy Spirit from me. Restore to me the joy of Your salvation, and uphold me with a willing spirit.

Psalm 51:10–12

# Lifted Up

Dear God,

Thank You for bringing me back to You after I stray. I was late to work today and fudged a little bit on my time sheet. But I knew it was wrong. I worried about it for half the day and finally realized that I had to be honest. I didn't need to let a lie take over my thoughts again. So I corrected the time sheet and told my boss I was late. I let her know that I didn't have a good reason. I was tired and slept too late.

My boss was understanding, but she did warn me to be on time from now on.

What happened the rest of the day surprised me. I wasn't worried. I didn't fret about being found out. I felt confident and on task. I was less stressed out.

It was a relief to be honest. It was a blessing to be brought back from slipping into a lie. I know I have to take responsibility for my actions, but having the issues out in the open feels so much better than living in hiding.

Thank You for lifting me up when I fell down. Thank You for showing Your love and mercy to me through my boss. Thank You for being my faithful leader, helper, and friend.

## Something to think about

I lift up my eyes to the mountains—where does my help come from? My help comes from the Lord, the Maker of heaven and earth. He will not let your foot slip—He who watches over you will not slumber.

Psalm 121:1–3 NIV

# It's Not About Me

## Dear God,

My mentor was very helpful to me today. During lunch we talked about what I can say when I have a difficult truth to confess. She let me know that it is never easy to be honest about a failure or a disappointing action. How true that is!

It's easy to be honest when everything to report is good. My challenge is to speak the truth when I have to admit my own sins and errors. I have a hard time being honest when I feel threatened or when I think I'm going to lose out on something. That's when I'm tempted to speak a half-truth, or withhold the truth, or gossip, or keep money I'm not supposed to have, or exaggerate facts in an untruthful way, or cheat, or plagiarize. This list can go on. It's the pressure situations that challenge me most.

My mentor talked to me about God's faithfulness. She reminded me that I don't have to be afraid of what I perceive as personal loss or disappointment from others. I can trust God's faithfulness. Even when I experience the consequences of my actions, I can trust God to be faithful. He will use my honesty to show His faithfulness to others.

What I've learned is that this is not all about me. It's about showing people in my life that God's faithfulness is real and that His truth is a beautiful thing. Even when I am weak, He will help me live in that truth.

## Something to think about

Likewise the Spirit helps us in our weakness. For we do not know what to pray for as we ought, but the Spirit Himself intercedes for us with groanings too deep for words.

Romans 8:26

# My Real Mission

Dear God,

Thank You for opening my eyes to the real purpose of honesty. It's all about showing Your grace and truth to the world. I see now that dishonesty is the natural course of a sinful world. It's so easy to get caught up in that untruthful flow. But You want the world to know something much better.

My pastor pointed out something very interesting. He said that Jesus started many of His sentences with the words, "Truly I say to you," or "I tell you the truth." Jesus was doing something very different from the world's ways. He brought the Good News of God's love to us. He made very clear that God's right way is the best way—and it is a way of grace and truth for us.

Thank You for showing me that I can be a part of bringing Your important truth to the world. My actions of honesty shine Your light to others. I pray that You would bring to my mind the words of Jesus before I speak and act. May the words "I tell You the truth" mark my life and show Your grace and faithfulness to everyone.

You have taught me that my real mission goes even deeper than personal honesty. It is to represent You and share the Good News of salvation with all. Thank You for that significant purpose and for using my humble life as an instrument of Your grace.

### Something to think about

Therefore, we are ambassadors for Christ, God making His appeal through us. We implore you on behalf of Christ, be reconciled to God. For our sake He made Him to be sin who knew no sin, so that in Him we might become the righteousness of God.

2 Corinthians 5:20–21

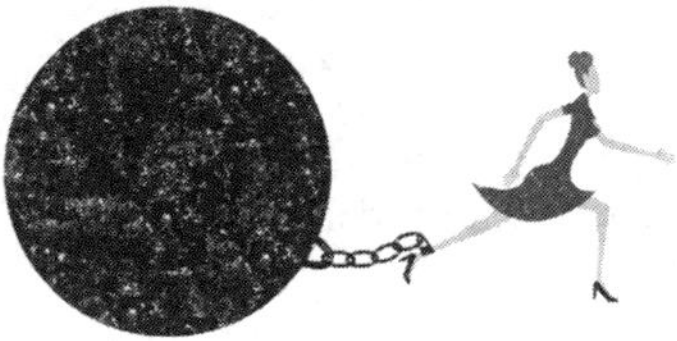

# Silence

Dear God,

I am learning the value of silence. I'm finding peace in not making excuses, not trying to cover my tracks, not trying to be someone I'm not, and not trying to gain an advantage. Instead, it is so freeing simply to be still.

As I reflect on this journey, I realize that my dishonesty was coming from a lack of contentment and gratitude. I was always trying to be liked by everyone, accepted by people, or affirmed by others. I was on a quest to look better, to outdo another person, and to find the next temporary pleasure. It all led to dishonesty.

But Your love is changing all that. You give me what I need for each day. You teach me to be thankful for the blessings in my life. Being Your beloved child lets me know that I don't have to strive for affirmation all the time. I can be content in any and every situation because Jesus gives me His love and strength.

I have much growing to do. I also have to mend some fences and prove I'm trustworthy to people close to me. But I will take one day at a time to live in Your love, to give thanks for Your kindness, and to love others as You have loved me. I will be quiet and let You lead me in truth.

### Something to think about

"Be still, and know that I am God."

Psalm 46:10

# Teach Me

Dear God,

You have shown me that You are strong and caring. You have shown me how much You love me. You have forgiven me and have given me hope in my Savior, Jesus.

Please accept my gratitude for Your love. You've rescued me from the dizzying gyrations of dishonesty. You have prepared a new path for me through the help of family and friends. Now You teach me daily to live in Your truth.

Please continue to strengthen me through Your Word. Keep teaching me through the godly people You have placed in my life. Keep reinforcing the blessings of honesty as I face temptations to fall into dishonesty again. Please make me a consistent person of truth.

You are my strength. I will listen to You and follow You. I celebrate Your love and the new life You give me. Please keep shaping my life Your way.

## Something to think about

I have chosen the way of faithfulness; I set Your rules before me. I cling to Your testimonies, O Lord; let me not be put to shame! I will run in the way of Your commandments when You enlarge my heart!

Psalm 119:30–32

# General Prayers

## Lord's Prayer

Our Father, who art in heaven, hallowed be Thy name, Thy kingdom come, Thy will be done on earth as it is in heaven. Give us this day our daily bread; and forgive us our trespasses as we forgive those who trespass against us; and lead us not into temptation, but deliver us from evil. For Thine is the kingdom and the power and the glory forever and ever. Amen.

## Morning Prayer

I thank You, my heavenly Father, through Jesus Christ, Your dear Son, that You have kept me this night from all harm and danger; and I pray that You would keep me this day also from sin and every evil, that all my doings and life may please You. For into Your hands I commend myself, my body and soul, and all things. Let Your holy angel be with me, that the evil foe may have no power over me. Amen.

## Evening Prayer

I thank You, my heavenly Father, through Jesus Christ, Your dear Son, that You have graciously kept me this day; and I pray that You would forgive me all my sins where I have done wrong, and graciously keep me this night. For into Your hands I commend myself, my body and soul, and all things. Let Your holy angel be with me, that the evil foe may have no power over me. Amen.

## For Control of the Tongue

We pray You, O Lord, to keep our tongues from evil and our lips from speaking deceit, that as Your holy angels continuously sing praises to You in heaven, so may we at all times glorify You on earth; through Jesus Christ, our Lord. (*LSB*, p. 312)

## For Mercy

Lord, You have searched me and You know me! You know when I sit down and when I stand up; even from a distance You know my very thoughts. You know what I have put my hands to during the day and the content of my dreams at night. You are acquainted with all my ways. Alas, You know also how often I have sinned against You this day, how often I have transgressed Your holy Law, and how often I have failed to keep my promises of loyalty to You and Your Word. Lord do not enter into judgment against Your servant. Do not deal with me in accordance with my sin, and do not give me the just reward for my iniquities, but rather graciously blot out all my trespasses for the sake of Your own Son, in whose blood I have redemption and the forgiveness of sins. As the night darkens around me, I again come to You for Your gracious protection, firmly trusting that You will keep Your child safe from all danger of body and soul. Grant to me and all Your children refreshing sleep, so that with renewed energy we may awake to serve You in our daily vocation; in Jesus' name. Amen. (*Lutheran Book of Prayer*, p. 17)

# Suggested Scripture Readings

Finally, brothers, whatever is true, whatever is honorable, whatever is just, whatever is pure, whatever is lovely, whatever is commendable, if there is any excellence, if there is anything worthy of praise, think about these things. What you have learned and received and heard and seen in me—practice these things, and the God of peace will be with you.

Philippians 4:8–9

And Jesus answered them, "Those who are well have no need of a physician, but those who are sick. I have not come to call the righteous but sinners to repentance."

Luke 5:31–32

God shows His love for us in that while we were still sinners, Christ died for us.

Romans 5:8

Create in me a clean heart, O God, and renew a right spirit within me. Cast me not away from Your presence, and take not Your Holy Spirit from me. Restore to me the joy of Your salvation, and uphold me with a willing spirit.

Psalm 51:10–12

If we confess our sins, He is faithful and just to forgive us our sins and to cleanse us from all unrighteousness.

1 John 1:9

[Jesus] said to me, "My grace is sufficient for you, for My power is made perfect in weakness." Therefore I will boast all the more gladly of my weaknesses, so that the power of Christ may rest upon me.

2 Corinthians 12:9